RAID ON THE INARTICULATE

POEMS BY
DEEPAK CHOPRA

HAY HOUSE

Carlsbad, California • New York City
London • Sydney • New Delhi

Published in the United Kingdom by:
Hay House UK Ltd, The Sixth Floor, Watson House,
54 Baker Street, London W1U 7BU
Tel: +44 (0)20 3927 7290; Fax: +44 (0)20 3927 7291; www.hayhouse.co.uk

Published in the United States of America by:
Hay House Inc., PO Box 5100, Carlsbad, CA 92018-5100
Tel: (1) 760 431 7695 or (800) 654 5126
Fax: (1) 760 431 6948 or (800) 650 5115; www.hayhouse.com

Published in Australia by:
Hay House Australia Ltd, 18/36 Ralph St, Alexandria NSW 2015
Tel: (61) 2 9669 4299; Fax: (61) 2 9669 4144; www.hayhouse.com.au

Published in India by:
Hay House Publishers India, Muskaan Complex, Plot No.3, B-2,
Vasant Kunj, New Delhi 110 070
Tel: (91) 11 4176 1620; Fax: (91) 11 4176 1630; www.hayhouse.co.in

Project editor: Anna Cooperberg
Cover design: Julie Davison • *Interior design:* Bryn Starr Best

Previously published by Infinite Possibilities Products, L.L.C., first printing 1996
Hardcover ISBN: 1-8829-71-16-7

A catalogue record for this book is available from the British Library.

Tradepaper ISBN: 978-1-78817-826-6
E-book ISBN: 978-1-4019-6907-3

Printed and bound by CPI Group (UK) Ltd, Croydon, CR0 4YY

RAID
ON THE
INARTICULATE

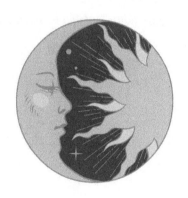

ALSO BY DEEPAK CHOPRA

*Power, Freedom, and Grace**

*The Seven Spiritual Laws of Success**

Total Meditation

You Are the Universe (with Menas C. Cafatos PhD)

Metahuman

The Healing Self (with Rudolph E. Tanzi PhD)

Super Genes (with Rudolph E. Tanzi PhD)

Quantum Healing

Perfect Health

CONTENTS

MAGICAL BEGINNINGS

FOREWORD

Ever since I was a child, I was drawn to poetry. My grandmother would recite to me sacred verses from the mythic traditions of India where gods and goddesses frolicked in celestial playgrounds. Mystery, magic, wonder, and enchantment expressed in verse became the raw materials of my imagination. Later in my childhood, I was introduced to the poems of Kabir, Rumi, and Tagore who, through rhythm and rhyme, brought to me a sacred world I knew existed, and was real and yet beyond my reach in the world of everyday reality. It was, nonetheless, a world that my soul yearned for . . . the agony of wishing and not finding.

As I grew up, I came across the poems of Emily Dickinson, D. H. Lawrence, Lord Byron, Percy Bysshe Shelley, Samuel Coleridge, William Blake, William Shakespeare, Geoffrey Chaucer, and Alfred, Lord Tennyson. I began to understand the meaning and effect of onomatopoeia, where the sound echoes the sense and where just the recitation of songs, ballads, and poems can lift you out of everyday existence, transporting you to higher states of awareness.

Even today if I close my eyes to hear the exquisite verse of Tennyson's "Morte d'Arthur" from *Idylls of the King*, I can see on the screen of my consciousness and hear through the stereophonic sound system of my imagination . . . the clash of armies on the Isle of Avalon. I can sense the crunch of ice as the armored heels of King Arthur and his brave, wounded knights trudge across the snow of England.

Look at the following words and see for yourself how your physiology reacts to the nostalgia of a bygone era.

Dry clash'd his harness in the icy caves
And barren chasms, and all to left and right
The bare black cliff clang'd round him, as he based
His feet on juts of slippery crag that rang
Sharp-smitten with the dint of armed heels—
And on a sudden, lo! the level lake,
And the long glories of the winter moon.

Even now as I read these lines, I am taken inexplicably to a world that I've only experienced in the imagination but always longed to know.

Poetry is—in the words of T.S. Eliot—a "raid on the inarticulate." This is because poetry, like meditation, allows us to slip into the gap between thoughts and get in touch with the karmic software of our souls. Here are insights and epiphanies, revelations, and a world of enchantment, such as we have never dreamed of in our ordinary waking state of consciousness.

The following selection of poems is an offering from my heart. I hope that as you read them you will be inspired to sing your own song.

Author's Note

The poems are strongly influenced by some of my spiritual mentors, such as Rabindranath Tagore, Jelaluddin Rumi, and others. In a few poems, I have directly borrowed a phrase or two from them.

"Ladies turning pages of poetry with indolent hands" was a sentiment expressed by W.B. Yeats in his introduction to *Gitanjali.*

"The inscrutable without name and form" was a phrase that Tagore frequently used to refer to God, as were phrases like "the lap of deathless spirit" and "the seashore of endless worlds."

In the poem "Body, brain, mind, and spirit," there are two lines where I have paraphrased Robert Frost's famous expression, "We dance round in a ring and suppose, But the secret sits in the middle and knows."

In the poem "We have met before" stanza four says, "We have been the plantation of sugar cane, and eaten its sweetness too." This is a direct paraphrase of a sentiment expressed by Jelaluddin Rumi.

SONGS
TO
MYSELF

PRISONER OF WORDS

Spells, charms, incantations

Be careful what you say…

The magic of words enfolds intention

Centuries of knowledge

Layers of experience, an entire history

In a few syllables.

Our lifetime is packaged inside us

As imprints triggered by words.

Wrapped in words the way a

Spider wraps flies in gossamer

We are both the spider and the fly

Imprisoning ourselves in our own web.

LOVE

Love is the spark in my heart.

Love is the light of the cosmos,

A raging flame that devours

Sun, moon and stars.

Love is the air we breathe.

It is not pleasure or even ecstasy

It is not emotion or feeling

Love is the circulation in every cell

Love is invisible and ever-present

Love is the only power.

Its universal force permeates everything

It does not possess, control or dominate

If you want love, place no conditions.

TITANIC FORCES

I gaze upon the night sky

    Looking at the flow of time

    Nurturing every small step

    The organization of the first hydrogen atom

    The formation of stars

    The birth of DNA

    Out of randomness

    Titanic forces swirl through the cosmos

    Order, evolution, balance, intelligence

    This is the force of spirit

    This is the crest of the wave of life

    This is the surge of love that makes me

    A privileged child of the universe

I MUST MAKE PEACE WITH MY SHADOWS

I am fragmented and conflicted

By so many personalities

Competing for the use of my body.

Sinners and saints are arguing

Forbidden lust and unconditional love

Divine and diabolical

The beatitude of paradise

Dark night of the soul.

Each of these have staked a claim

Shouting over each other

Causing endless trouble

Inside me saying "yes" and "no"

Guilt and shame have been implanted

and I have become stained with fear

The secret caverns and dark cells of my psyche

are riddled with doubt and shame

I have become the keeper of my shadow selves

The prisoner of my own jail

Tapping messages on the wall of my cell.

I have held on to negative energies,

Forgotten the instinct for release.

I'm a loaded battery of anger,

resentment and frustration.

I'm a bomb.

Bombs blow up and kill people.

The explosion of shrapnel is the

explosion of rage.

I must make peace with my shadows,

Bring this war to an end.

JOURNEY TO MY BEING

I am living as a finite package of flesh and bone.

In thin wedges of space and time

I have become solid stuff

Atoms of carbon and hydrogen

and oxygen and nitrogen.

I must make a journey in the quest for alchemy

Beneath the surface of atoms and molecules

Behind the appearance of change.

I must quest beyond the boundless,

Beyond the boundaries of bone, muscle,

tissue and cell.

I must ride the crest of these clouds of energies

Beyond the play of light and shadow.

I must peel the layers of my soul

Arriving at the timeless core

At the center of my being.

SURRENDER

Swirling atoms of oxygen
   enter my blood with every breath.

   Teeming enzymes and proteins are
   the tide and flood of my cells.

   Electrical neuronal storms never cease.
   They blast and echo in the endless
   corridors of my mind.

   Is this chaos another face of order?

   The same tugs of gravity that created dancing stars
   are holding these miniscule strands of DNA,
   enfolding and unfolding the memories of
   evolutionary time.

We are fooled by appearances

Uncertainty is my doorway to freedom

I gave become unpredictable and odd.

Thinking, deciding, choosing and feeling

I offer these to the automatic side of my brain.

And at last, after eons of struggle and pain

I am learning to surrender to God

I am alive now.

TICKET TO FREEDOM

I have projected the same images day after day

Becoming a prisoner of the known.

But the known is dead and past now

And I must buy my ticket to freedom

By embracing the fresh unknown.

Chance encounters, unexpected coincidences

Premonitions, dreams and wishes

Flashes of unpredictable joy

Random events are

Weaving themselves in the web of time.

I have left the voice of reason.

I am listening to the beckoning whisper

In the recesses of my heart.

And new shapes of reality

Are coaxing me out of my prison.

HIDDEN TREASURES

Aware of myself

Simply as myself

In my knowingness

I embraced death

And caught her

in my arms like a lover.

In my death was my certainty of existence

Never to be born, never to cease to be,

Whatever I had lost was temporary and unreal.

When I looked in the ashes

In the rubble of devastation and disorder,

there were buried hidden treasures.

SPIRIT SPEAKS

Beyond opposites of light and dark

    I exist

    Beyond good and evil, pleasure and pain.

    Everything I see has roots in the unseen world

    Nature reflects my moods

    The body and mind may sleep,

    I am always awake.

    I possess the secret of immortality.

    Living in the midst of birth and death

    I pervade all the layers of reality.

    Infinite worlds come and go

    in the vast expanse of my consciousness.

    I exist simultaneously in all times

    Creating endless versions of every event

    Moment by moment

    I have woven the fragile threads of time

    Spinning the boundless web

    of eternity.

RECYCLED DUST

The fine sand slipping through my fingers so fast

This call from past, this quiet dust,

Is pyramids and castles and cities that did not last.

It is pharaohs, generals and beauty queens

Conspiracies, secrets and things unseen.

It is loving, passion, suffering, pain

The blood of Christ, his guts, his breath, his brain.

It is tragedy, comedy, lightening, thunder,

earthquake and storm

This raging cyclone of phenomenon and form.

Lessons of history, ancient lore

Clashing armies, death and gore

This quiet dust is the birth of stars

Titanic forces and a lonely asteroid

Elements, particles, and spiraling galaxies

in the infinite void

Queen of Sheba, Mohammed and Cleopatra

Forgiveness of God and judgment hereafter.

Laughter, crying, courage, fear

Thinking, thought, scenery, seer,

Villain and foe, hero and clown

The silent dust is everything we see

Disguising itself, it's you and me

INVISIBLE
FORCES

AGELESS BODY, TIMELESS MIND

Don't ask why,

    Waves of energy bind you and me

    to spring flowers and birds that fly.

    To rushing brook and ocean wide

    To divine beings and angels by our side.

    To pre-quantum regions without dimension

    From before the Fall and after the Ascension.

    From before the big bang and after the universe ends

    in the heat death of absolute zero.

    Privileged children of the cosmos

    Nothing is separate from you.

    Deep inside the fabric of matter and energy

    There are gods and goddesses in embryo

    waiting to be born.

Flowing, flexible, dynamic, fresh

Ever-renewing, timeless, innocent,

Full of wonder, ever-guileless

Your body is the body of the universe

Uni-verse, one song.

A dizzying entry into the dance of life

Effortless, spontaneous, without struggle or strife

Where dancers disappear

If your approach is too near.

And the music fades away

Into the silence of eternity.

We join the fraternity

Where nothing is separate from you.

And deep inside the fabric

Of matter and energy

There are gods and goddesses in embryo

Waiting to be born.

You are not your atoms

They come and go

You are not your thoughts

They come and go

You are not your images

Your fierce, fearful ego

You are above and beyond these

You are the witness, the interpreter,

The self beyond all images.

You are ageless and timeless.

BODY, BRAIN, MIND AND SPIRIT

Verbal cues, fed to us in early childhood,

Still run inside our heads

Like muffled tape loops.

Words, concepts, molecules, matter.

Images, symbols,

triggers for biological transformation.

Information

In form ation

Body brain mind and spirit.

Spirit, mind, body, brain

Pleasure, pain, loss, and gain

Sunshine, rain.

Are inextricably woven,

As the warp and woof

Of our lives.

Sistine Chapel, Paradise Lost

Pyramids, castles

Palaces, monuments, Taj Mahal

You stand as mute witness to

the choreographer who invented

every step of the dance.

She was there, you never saw her.

You were not looking,

Never had a chance.

Lost in words

Images concepts

running inside your head

Like muffled tape loops

Obscure the silence

Between the notes.

The secret that sits on center stage and knows

While we dance around our lives and suppose

Body brain mind and spirit.

Spirit, mind, body, brain

Pleasure, pain, loss and gain

Sunshine, rain.

Are inextricably woven,

As the warp and woof

Of our lives.

CREATIVE IMPULSES OF THE COSMOS

The mind of God.

Where does it hide?

Creative impulses of the cosmos,

Where do you abide?

In the depths of your soul are

Boundless energies and

Powerful forces, side by side.

Infinite accomplishments with little effort.

In the eternal storehouse of creation

Are treasures beyond imagination.

Invisible forces are here to help you

They are silent outside the bounds of fear.

Step aside, do not interfere.

Look within and face the world.

In the mirror of relationships

Are secrets to be unfurled.

Wherever you go, there you are.

In this realm there is no near or far...

A speck of dirt on planet Earth

A cloud of gas on distant Mars.

A flame of candle or

Dancing light on distant stars.

There are worlds that come and go,

Like motes of dust in space and time

In this body you will not find

The me, that's free, a different kind.

In this world and not of it,

You will understand, bit by bit.

Behind the machinations of history,

Lurks a deeper mystery.

Fearless, magnificent, full of splendour.

You must enter it, naked and in surrender.

The mind of God.

Where does it hide?

Creative impulses of the cosmos,

Where do you abide?

In the depths of your soul

Are boundless energies and

Powerful forces, side by side.

MAGICAL
BEGINNINGS

MAGICAL BEGINNINGS

Magical beginnings and enchanted lives

The birth of stars, planet earth

Your home, your place

You come to us from the void of space

Visions of gods in the endless void

Journeying along this lonely asteroid

Darling child give us your joy

So all on earth may be healed and holy

Floating down the stream of eternity

You are becoming our destiny.
You are becoming our destiny.

I REJOICE IN YOUR COMING

I rejoice in your coming

Child of mine

The elements have fashioned you

Over eons of time.

Child of the universe

You are more than you seem

A wistful memory

God's dream.

Centuries of experience and desires

And yearnings have created you

Lifesongs of ages have burst into

Melodies eternally new.

I've seen in your movements

And the pulse of your heart

The dance of the cosmos

From finish to start.

The throb of your life

Coursing through my blood

Is the ebb and flow of

The tide and the flood.

Child of the universe and child of mine

I rejoice in your coming.

On the seashore of tiwme

For a night and a day

We will meet soon and have our play.

Child of the universe

We will laugh and we will cry

But I promise you darling

We will never sigh.

You have a purpose,

A dream in your soul.

In fulfilling your dharma.

You will make life whole.

I rejoice in your coming,

Child of mine.

The elements have fashioned you

Over eons of time.

CREATING A NEW WORLD

Ah, ancient one

That fire can not burn

Water can not wet,

Wind can not dry,

Weapons can not cleave.

Your soul of unblemished joy,

Spirit of unbounded love,

Has danced and cascaded

And cavorted and rippled

Across the vast ocean of consciousness

And stranded on my heart and in my life.

You are supremely concentrated sweetness,

Wonder, curiosity and alertness.

You are truth, integrity, honesty and trust.

You are hope, compassion,

Peace, harmony and laughter.

You are beauty.

Courage is your essence,

Free of memories and anticipations.

The universe has conspired to create you,

Child of the universe

Child of mine.

You are eternal

Taking birth in time.

You are the supreme being

Creating a new world.

BLISSFUL BABY

Blissful baby

who are you?

Where have you come from?

Blissful baby

you have waited patiently

since the dawn of creation.

Through turbulent tempests

and misty clouds

and violent storms

you have floated down the ages

hiding yourself in the shadows

from the womb of creation

from the lap of deathless spirit

who rules the world

the formless ocean of infinity.

You now come to this playhouse of infinite forms.

Blissful baby,

song of the cosmos

privileged child of the universe

we will love you and nurture you,

feed you, clothe you, play with you.

We are travelers together on the endless journey,

we have met for a moment

on the highway of eternity.

You are blessed and blesséd are we

the inscrutable without name and form

has brought us together.

Privileged child of the universe, let us sing our song

I KNOW YOU MY CHILD

I know you my child

you are coming to us

you have been a lover so many times

A lover in life

A lover in death

A lover in the tomb

A lover from the day of resurrection

A lover in paradise

A lover forever

My love, my heart, my purest essence

you are the force that will transform this world

Agony will become ecstasy and

the secret longings of my soul

will blaze a fire

that will make us whole.

Child of the Universe,
You Are Becoming Mine

It is in the unknown that we live and move

and you, the unknown, are becoming known to me

endless versions of infinity are being precipitated

into versions of time

you are the prophet

you are the god.

My darling child,

I await your becoming from being

with bated breath.

Child of the universe,

you are becoming mine.

SACRED BEING

Sacred being you came as a gift from the universe.

You are made from the dust of the ground,

And spirit has breathed into you

The breath of life.

You have become a living soul.

I honor and worship you.

All my wishes and dreams

My hopes, my aspirations, my longings

And wistful yearnings are embodied in your form

You are the infinite treasure house of formless
eternity

I will love you with the force and energy of god.

You are the immeasurable potential of all

That was and is and will be

The realm of infinite possibility.

Sacred being,

Your throb of life fills me with ecstasy,

Mystery overwhelms me

When I think of your coming.

Sacred being,

You are made from the dust of the ground

And spirit has breathed into you the breath of life

So you have become a living soul

A gift from the unknown.

You are the seed of desire

Life of my life

seed of my essence

you are the seed of desire

my darling.

It was through desire that the unmanifest

made link with the manifest.

Through desire the invisible was made visible

Through desire the spirit became this body

born of dust

So wondrous to behold.

As is your desire my child,

so is your intention.

As is your intention,

so is your will.

As is your will,

so is your destiny.

You are the seed of enchanted forests

and of mystical realms

Together we will nurture our desires

in the sacred corridors of our souls

One day these desires will burst into flame

and in the burnished glow

and sudden splendour of love

we will dream a new world of reality

from the purity of our hearts.

WE HAVE MET BEFORE

We have met before

    perhaps you have forgotten

    the tea we shared

    on the bridge of rope

    by the river

    near the waterfall

    by the mountain

    in Tibet.

    Or maybe it was Covent Garden,

    in the England of Dickens or Yeats

    while the ladies sipped champagne

    turning pages of poetry

    with indolent hands.

    Remember those days

    in those heavy mists of time?

    You were father and I was child.

And so we keep reversing roles

playing out these games of life

father, son, mother, child,

lover, beloved, sinner, saint,

victor, vanquished

seer and scenery.

We have been the plantation of sugar cane,

and eaten its sweetness too.

Our destinies have been intertwined

playing out these versions, ever-new,

as we unscroll these pages of time.

I am you and you are me,

and all is one,

me and mine.

We have met before

perhaps you have forgotten

the tea we shared

on the bride of rope

by the river

near the waterfall

by the mountain

in Tibet.

ONCE I WAS A CHILD
AND DID CHILDISH THINGS

Once I was a child and did childish things

On the seashores of endless worlds I had my play,

I made and unmade my gods with worthless clay.

Once we were children and did childish things.

We carelessly frolicked on forgotten shores

dust in the dust, wind in the wind,

and though the waters were turbulent

stars and moon were mirrored in our being.

In love with life we lived the sweetest of passions,

We lived like gypsies and children of God.

Now we are grown and the wonder is gone.

Gone is the laughter, the adventure, the mystery.

My darling, my child, my teacher, my god-in-embryo

I await your manifestation with passion sublime.

Once again we will frolic on the sand of time.

THE PRIMORDIAL ONE

You are the earth, wind, and fire,

You are the void of space

and the deep waters.

You are the sun, moon and dust of stars

Gestating over millennia in the crucible of creation.

you have come springing out of nothingness

bringing the entire universe with you.

You are vid, vard, word, idea and veda…

Pure knowledge, pure intelligence

Pure essence

Divinity in motion.

You are macrocosm in microcosm

Cosmic body in human body

Cosmic mind in human mind.

Truly, you are god in embryo,

The generator, organizer

and deliverer of existence.

The total mind.

As you appear within our midst

with the sudden splendour of your magnificent being

you bring us to the sacred core of our existence

the sacrament, the covenant,

the agreement we had

that you the creator

would ever be present

and in every grain of creation.

Now I realise you were always here

and we were not looking

with eyes purified

and the mind of soul

awake once again in beams of light.

I see you in rainbows

and clouds and blades of grass

in dolphins dancing on the ocean.

In sunshine

In rain

In snows of winter

In ripened grain

In falling autumn leaves.

Omnipresent, omnipotent, omniscient.

Oh mighty one

the ancient inscrutable without name or form

Brahman, Abraham, The Primordial One.

You have come to us as this gift of child

salutations, salutations to you a million times.

You Create Again and Again

Ever-present, all-pervading
all knowing, eternal, causeless.
Bigger than the biggest
smaller than the small
you begin your journey as
a speck of information in DNA.

Food, sound, music, image, thought,
feeling, emotion, desire, memory,
transform you into
eye, nostril, ear, brain, body
organ, cell, tissue, muscle and bone.

You are ever renewing yourself
as form and phenomenon.
Through this child
you are becoming conscious,
once again, of yourself.

Through myriad eyes,
You see yourself.

Through countless ears

you hear yourself.

Through endless mouths

You eat yourself.

Curving back within yourself

You create yourself

Again and again.

You are the slayer and the slain,

You are the creator and the creation,

The seer and the seen.

Behold this child.

From the womb of creation,

to the seed of man,

to the womb of woman,

you have come again and again,

ever dancing

your cosmic dance.

ACKNOWLEDGMENTS

My dear friends and colleagues, Leon Nacson, Reid Tracy, and Patty Gift. Also to the Hay House team, Errin Dunn, Georgia Robertson, Rosie Barry, Betsy Beier, Anna Cooperberg, and Celeste Johnson.

ABOUT THE AUTHOR

DEEPAK CHOPRA™ is a world-renowned pioneer in integrative medicine and personal transformation. He is the founder of the Chopra Foundation, a non-profit entity for research on wellbeing and humanitarianism, and Chopra Global, a modern-day health company at the intersection of science and spirituality. Chopra is a clinical professor of Family Medicine and Public Health at the University of California San Diego, and serves as a senior scientist with Gallup Organization. He is the author of over 90 books translated into over 43 languages, including numerous *New York Times* bestsellers. www.deepakchopra.com

Hay House Titles of Related Interest

YOU CAN HEAL YOUR LIFE, the movie,
starring Louise Hay & Friends
(available an online streaming video)
www.hayhouse.com/louise-movie

THE SHIFT, the movie,
starring Dr Wayne W. Dyer
(available as an online streaming video)
www.hayhouse.com/the-shift-movie

DESIGNING DESTINY: Heartfulness Practices to Find Your Purpose and Fulfill Your Potential, by Kamlesh D. Patel

EVERYTHING IS HERE TO HELP YOU:
A Loving Guide to Your Soul's Evolution, by Matt Kahn

INTIMATE CONVERSATIONS WITH THE DIVINE:
Prayer, Guidance, and Grace, by Caroline Myss

UNBLOCKED: A Revolutionary Approach to Tapping into Your Chakra Empowerment Energy to Reclaim Your Passion, Joy, and Confidence, by Margaret Lynch Raniere and David Raniere, Ph.D.

THE WISDOM CODES:
Timeless Truths from Masters of Change,
by Gregg Braden

All of the above are available at www.hayhouse.co.uk